ISLINGTON

12/17

Please return this item on or before the last date stamped below or you may be liable to overdue charges. To renew an item call the number below, or access the online catalogue at www.islington.gov.uk/libraries. You will need your library membership number and PIN number.

Islington Libraries

020 7527 6900   **www.islington.gov.uk/libraries**

EDGE
BOOKS

SPORTS TO THE EXTREME

EXTREME
Snow AND Ice
Sports

BY ERIN K BUTLER

raintree

a Capstone company — publishers for children

Raintree is an imprint of Capstone Global Library Limited, a company incorporated in England and Wales having its registered office at 264 Banbury Road, Oxford, OX2 7DY – Registered company number: 6695582

www.raintree.co.uk
myorders@raintree.co.uk

Edited by Nikki Ramsay
Designed by Sara Radka
Production by Laura Manthe

ISBN 978-1-4747-4790-5 (library binding)
22 21 20 19 18 17
10 9 8 7 6 5 4 3 2 1

British Library Cataloguing in Publication Data
A full catalogue record for this book is available from the British Library.

Acknowledgements
Getty Images: Christopher Bernard, 9, Cultura RF, 13, Westend61, 25, iStockphoto, cover, 1, Jan Hetfleisch/Bongarts, 21, Joerg Mitter/Red Bull, 26, Sebastian Marko/Red Bull, 27; Newscom: Hiroyuki Sato/AFLO, 6, ZUMAPRESS/Greg Smith, 15, ZUMAPRESS/Joel Marklund/Bildbyran, 19, Dave Phillips/MCT, 22; Shutterstock: Alessandro Colle, 5, divedog, 28, Dmytro Vietrov, 6, IM_photo, 11, Mark Bonham, 17, Tyler Meade Photography, 18, YanLev, 7

Graphic elements by Book Buddy Media.

Contents

Extreme snow & ice sports

When the weather turns cold and the ground is covered with ice and snow, most people like to stay inside. These can be **treacherous** conditions. But there is one group of people that love this environment – extreme ice and snow enthusiasts.

Extreme snow and ice sports are physically demanding activities. They involve high speed and high risk, and are performed on snow or icy **terrain**. These sports depend on natural landscapes and the weather to create the perfect extreme environment. With slippery surfaces, snow-covered hills and biting cold, snow and ice sports are in a class of their own.

Most extreme winter sports require special equipment. Some are performed on boards. Some use carefully designed machinery. And others require tools specifically for ice. No matter the tools or equipment involved, snow and ice sports are some of the world's most extreme activities.

treacherous – marked by danger and difficulty

terrain – the surface of the land

Ice climbers need to know as much as they can about the ice conditions before they start climbing.

Extreme snowboarders can ride either on a halfpipe or in the natural environment.

EXTREME(LY) YOUNG

Some of the world's best extreme athletes participate in a competition called the X Games. The X Games are held in both the summer and the winter.

In 2014 American snowboarder Chloe Kim won a silver medal at the X Games. She was the youngest athlete to ever win a medal at the competition. Since then, she has become the only X Games athlete to win three gold medals before the age of 16.

CHAPTER 1

Extreme snowboarding

Snowboarders slide down snowy slopes at high speeds while strapped to a board. Invented in the 1960s, snowboarding mixed parts of skateboarding and surfing to glide across the snow. The idea quickly became popular. People began snowboarding all over the world.

Snowboards vary in size to change their stability and manoeuvrability.

Some people snowboard for fun or as a hobby. But others take this sport to the extreme. They aim for high speeds. They perform tricks, stunts and impressive manoeuvres. The hills on which they snowboard usually have more difficult terrain. There may also be obstacles for snowboarders to navigate, such as cliffs and ravines.

A snowboard is similar to a skateboard, but it has no wheels. Snowboards are also longer. A snowboard is, on average, 1.5 metres (5 feet) long, while a skateboard is smaller at about 0.76 m (2.5 feet) long.

Snowboards can be made of wood, plastic or foam. Different designs do different things. In speed-snowboarding and racing, the board is stiff and has hard boots that strap to the board and offer support. Freestyle boards are flexible and have soft boots that strap to the board.

Extreme snowboarders enter competitions to showcase their creativity and skill. The three main categories of competition are alpine, freestyle and boardercross.

Alpine competitions are based on speed and skill. Snowboarders fly downhill as fast as possible while weaving between **gates**. Freestyle competitions are more creative, with snowboarders using a halfpipe to perform daring tricks. Judges score each routine to select the winner. In boardercross, four to six snowboarders race down a hill while performing jumps and navigating obstacles.

Alpine snowboarders use longer boards for greater speeds. Freestyle boards are shorter, making tricks easier to perform. Boardercross boards are somewhere in between.

Not all extreme snowboarders compete. Some simply enjoy reaching high speeds on their boards, or creating new tricks. Many share pictures or videos of their snowboarding online.

Some snowboarders like seeking out new trails with fresh snow. They often find untouched snow in **backcountry** areas off the main trails. If they are not careful, they run the risk of starting an avalanche by boarding.

gates – narrow poles with a flag attached

backcountry – an isolated area often at high altitude that is not marked by trails or patrolled by park rangers or other authorities

Snowboarders must be ready for wintry weather. They wear lots of layers, gloves and goggles for warmth.

SNOWBOARDING IN THE OLYMPICS

Many extreme sports are not included in the Olympics, but that is slowly changing. Snowboarding entered the Winter Olympics for the first time in 1998 in Nagano, Japan. The first Olympic snowboarders – both men and women – competed in giant **slalom** and halfpipe events. Boardercross and similar competitions were added to the Winter Games in 2010 and 2014.

slalom – a downhill race in which riders weave through sets of poles

CHAPTER 2

Extreme skiing

When you think about skiing, you might think of vacations or resorts. But this winter sport can get much more extreme than just gentle hills. At a ski resort, the most difficult hills might have slopes of around 30 to 40 degrees. In extreme skiing, skiers speed down slopes at an angle of at least 45 degrees – if not more. To make things more difficult, the slopes are usually not part of known pistes. The snow is ungroomed, and there may be patches of ice or rock underneath.

The sport developed because people wanted a bigger thrill. Over the years, it has changed to become even more exciting. With the right skis, skiers can reach speeds of more than 97 kilometres (60 miles) per hour. They also perform tricks and stunts.

It can be difficult to reach the slopes that are needed for extreme skiing. A chairlift might not be enough to get you to the top. Sometimes, the only way to get there is by helicopter.

Getting from place to place is not the only challenge in extreme skiing. There's a lot of risk involved too. Taking paths no one has been on before can lead to unpredictable results. Skiers have to make lightning-quick decisions to avoid obstacles, and there is always the risk of causing an avalanche. Probes are carried to skiers so they can test snow conditions. Every skier also carries a shovel to dig himself or herself out of an avalanche.

When skiers perform jumps at high speeds, they take the sport to its most extreme.

Extreme skiers usually do not ski alone. They need to be able to call for help in an emergency. If a skier does ski alone, a GPS device is a necessary piece of equipment. This helps emergency responders find them in case they are buried in snow.

CHAPTER 3

Snowkiting

In summer, many people love to go kitesurfing on the water. Kitesurfers travel across the waves on a board while being pulled by a large kite. Extreme winter sports enthusiasts liked the idea of kitesurfing, but they did not have access to bodies of water. Instead, they **adapted** the sport for snow. Snowkiting was born.

Advanced snowkiters aim for high speeds and big jumps. Regular snowkiters can reach speeds of 48 km (30 miles) per hour. However, advanced snowkiters can reach up to 113 km (70 miles) per hour. Deeper snow and larger kites add to the challenge.

There are different styles and sizes of kites that a snowkiter can choose. In general, kites used for snowkiting are smaller than those used for kitesurfing. This is because ice and snow have much less **friction** than water. It takes less energy to get a snowkiter moving.

Skis offer the snowkiter more control, while snowboards give an experience more like kitesurfing. The last and most essential piece of equipment for every snowkiter is a helmet, which protects them in case of a fall.

adapt – to change to fit into a new or different environment

friction – a force produced when two objects rub against each other; friction slows down objects

Most kites are soft and do not have hard frames.

CHAPTER 4

Snow kayaking

Extreme kayaking is a well-known summer sport. But what do boaters do in the winter? They take their boats to the slopes! Instead of travelling down a river, snow kayakers use a waxed boat to speed down steep, snowy slopes.

Sliding down the slopes in a snow kayak can feel like sledging. It comes with high risks and an adrenaline rush. Snow kayakers can reach speeds of up to 80 km (50 miles) per hour. Kayaks can be difficult to control at these high speeds. Even with paddles, which give them more control than just a regular sledge, steering can be hard.

Most snow kayakers go kayaking in the wilderness. In these areas, paths have not been set up. But there are also special areas that have been set aside specifically for snow kayak racing.

AVALANCHE!

Many athletes who participate in extreme snow sports run the risk of getting caught in an avalanche. An avalanche is a sudden, potentially deadly flow of snow. The worst avalanches can travel as fast as 300 km (186 miles) per hour. Extreme winter sportspeople are especially at risk of starting an avalanche because they are disturbing new, heavy snow.

The Kayaks on Snow competition in Colorado, USA, sends athletes down snow-covered slopes and then into icy water to finish the race.

CHAPTER 5

Extreme snowmobiling

Snowmobiles are powerful vehicles. These sturdy machines often weigh around 200 kilograms (450 pounds). They are built to travel on rough, snowy terrain. A standard snowmobile has an engine, rubber tracks in the back, skis in the front, a seat and handlebars.

Originally, snowmobiles were used for transport or fun. Then, people began to realize that they could be used for a lot more. They started blazing their own trails in the wilderness. Jumps were built and tricks were performed. Motocross – but on snow – was born.

The two main types of extreme snowmobiling are freestyle and snocross. In freestyle, riders launch off ramps and get huge air of 30.5 m (100 feet) or more. They perform tricks while in the air, such as front flips, backflips and flashy landings.

Snocross riders try to reach the fastest speeds possible as they race against each other. Tracks include jumps, tight turns and obstacles. Riders have reached speeds of more than 160 km (100 miles) per hour.

EXTREME FACT!

In 1968 Ralph Plaisted and a group of adventurers became the first people to reach the North Pole on snowmobiles.

An essential part of a good snowmobile jump is the landing. The goal is to make it as smooth as possible.

Backcountry riding is a third type of extreme exploration. It is generally done for fun, not for competition. Snowmobilers ride in areas where no one has gone before. They love finding new places to ride. They are true trailblazers. But riders have to be very careful. Just like other mountain sports, there is a risk of avalanches.

Backcountry riders carry rucksacks full of survival gear. Radios, emergency food, first aid kits, whistles, tarpaulins and satellite phones are all on the must-have list.

TOP X GAMES SNOWMOBILING MOMENTS

Snocross is the oldest motorized X Games sport. Men and women compete separately in both snocross and freestyle events. They earn medals for racing and performing stunts. The X Games offer an opportunity for extreme snowmobilers to gather with other extreme winter athletes. They can show off their skills and learn from some of the best in their sport.

Over the years, snowmobilers have made their mark in the Winter X Games. In 2000 a snocross rider called Tucker Hibbert became the youngest person to win a gold medal in the winter games. He has won nine X Games gold medals since then. In 2011 brothers Caleb and Colten Moore performed a tandem backflip on a snowmobile. The next big challenge riders are tackling is a double backflip. The sky's the limit for extreme snowmobilers!

CHAPTER 6

Bobsleighing

Bobsleighing, also called bobsledding, is a sport in which racers speed down an ice-covered track. They use a vehicle called a bobsleigh. Bobsleighs are sleek and built to go as fast as possible. They can hold two or four riders. The rider in front is called the driver, while the rider in back is the brakeman or brakewoman. Riders in between are called the crew. Heavy bobsleighs can reach about 160 km (100 miles) per hour.

This extreme sport is an old one. It dates back to the 1880s. People began organizing and competing quickly. The first bobsleigh competition was held in 1898 in St Moritz, Switzerland. Bobsleighing was one of the first extreme Olympic sports. It was added in 1924.

It might not seem like bobsleighing requires much athleticism. But in reality, it is an incredibly difficult sport. It can also be dangerous, as bobsleighs are so heavy – up to 630 kg (1,389 pounds). Racers must be very strong to get the bobsleigh going from a stationary position. They run in spiked shoes to give the bobsleigh the best possible start. Then they must pull themselves into the moving bobsleigh. Riders work together to shift their weight and steer. Fractions of a second can mean the difference between winning and losing a race. Usually, bobsleighers are ranked based on their total time racing over four heats.

Bobsleighing courses are often around 1,500 m (4,920 feet) long, and include about 15 turns.

The longest running ski bike festival takes place in Durango, Colorado, in the United States. For more than 15 years, ski bikers have enjoyed a weekend of racing and community.

CHAPTER 7

Ski biking

Most people would never expect to see someone cycle through the snow. But, in the creative style of extreme sports, ski bikers have found a way. In ski biking, a rider sits on a bicycle-like frame. Instead of wheels, the bike has skis – one in the front and one in the back. The rider uses this unpowered vehicle to travel down the same slopes where other people ski.

Of all the extreme ice and snow sports, ski biking is one of the safest. The design of a ski bike makes it very stable. The first models were wooden and heavy. Over time, they have been improved to become much lighter. Many people use mountain bike and BMX frames.

The handlebars control the front ski. The back ski is controlled by the rider shifting his or her weight to the right or left.

Ski biking is a relatively new sport, and riders love coming up with creative ways to make it even more extreme. Flips, spins and jumps are just a few of the moves that extreme ski bikers are learning to perform.

EXTREME FACT!

Ski bikers can reach very high speeds when skiing downhill. The record stands at 222 km (138 miles) per hour.

CHAPTER 8

Ice climbing

Seasoned rock climbers know the thrill of conquering a mountainside. However, not all mountainsides are dirt and rock. Some are covered in ice and snow. In cold weather, extreme climbers ascend ice-covered rocks, glaciers and frozen waterfalls.

Ice climbing requires physical strength and special equipment. Climbers take their ice tools very seriously. These tools – ice axes, crampons and ice screws – can mean the difference between life and death. Ice axes have a pick on one side and an **adze** on the other. Crampons are spikes attached to the climber's shoes. They allow a climber to get **traction** on the ice. Ice screws help climbers in case of a fall. They are drilled into the ice and a rope is clipped to them. The rope attaches to the climber's harness.

Climbers develop different techniques depending on the angle of the ice. For example, flat footing is good for low angles, while front pointing works well for steep angles. The best ice climbers aim for fast speeds on tall, steep climbs. In 2015 Dani Arnold set a world speed record by climbing a 1,100-m (3,609-foot) wall of ice in 1 hour and 46 minutes.

adze – the flat, curved blade on an ice axe; climbers use the adze to chop ice and cut steps

traction – the amount of grip one surface has while moving over another surface

CHAPTER 9

Ice cross downhill

Ice skaters have gone extreme too. Ice cross downhill sets skaters against each other as they race at high speeds. They have to navigate drops, turns and obstacles. The first skater to the finish line wins.

In ice cross downhill competitions, skaters participate in races throughout the season to gain points. The skater with the most points at the end of the season is the world champion.

Ice cross downhill skaters can reach speeds of 80 km (50 miles) per hour. Races can become cutthroat as competitors rush for the finish.

The first ice cross downhill competition took place in 2001. Since then tracks have been built through cities and down mountains. Each track is filled with treacherous obstacles designed to challenge each racer. Tracks can be as long as 600 m (1,969 feet). Only the best skaters can tackle them. Head and body protection is a must.

Every year ice cross track designers work to make new tracks even more extreme.

Ice cross downhill races take place all over the world.

Many of the most popular ice diving locations are in Canada and Russia.

CHAPTER 10

Ice diving

One extreme winter sport does not involve speed, stunts or climbing. This sport is ice diving, a specialized form of scuba diving. To begin, a diver cuts a hole in the ice, which can be between 1.2 and 3 m (4 and 10 feet) thick. This is his or her only entry or exit point to the water. Using special equipment, the diver then enters the water and explores the depths.

Ice diving requires basic scuba diving training, but there's even more to it. Ice divers need to be able to withstand the frigid waters. Temperatures fall around minus 18 degrees Celsius (0 degrees Fahrenheit). They also must look for dangerous situations, such as unsafe ice conditions. Extreme cold can cause equipment to fail. In this dangerous environment, it is important that no equipment is left behind. A diver needs a drysuit for warmth, a knife and gauges to track their progress. Tethers ensure divers can make his or her way back to their original launch site.

Although ice diving is risky, it has huge benefits not seen anywhere else. Ice diving gives divers better visibility underwater. This can lead to some breathtaking sights. Ice divers get to see underwater rock and ice formations, light displays and rare sea life that regular scuba divers never see. Like so many extreme sports, dedicated training in ice diving leads to a great payoff.

Extreme snow and ice sports are some of the most creative and challenging in the world of extreme sports. As long as snow and ice exist, enthusiasts will be inventing new things and taking their sports to the extreme.

Glossary

adapt to change to fit into a new or different environment

adze the flat, curved blade on an ice axe; climbers use the adze to chop ice and cut steps

backcountry an isolated area often at high altitude that is not marked by trails or patrolled by park rangers or other authorities

friction a force produced when two objects rub against each other; friction slows down objects

gates narrow poles with a flag attached

slalom a downhill race in which riders weave through sets of poles

terrain the surface of the land

traction the amount of grip one surface has while moving over another surface

treacherous marked by danger and difficulty

Find out more

Extreme Downhill Ski Racing (Nailed It!), Virginia Loh-Hagan (45th Parallel Press, 2016)

Extreme Sports People (Celebrity Secrets), Paul Mason (Wayland, 2011)

Extreme Winter Sports (Extreme Games), Jim Brush (Franklin Watts, 2012)

Snowboard Cross (Extreme Winter Sports Zone), Darice Bailer (Lerner Publications, 2017)

Websites

http://www.ducksters.com/sports/extremesnowboarding.php

http://www.ducksters.com/sports/extremesnowmobile.php

http://kidshealth.org/en/kids/winter-sports.html

http://www.kidzworld.com/article/5168-skiing-101

https://www.teamgb.com/news/get-involved-how-get-winter-sports-uk

Index